The Last Lap

A SEQUENCE IN VERSE
ON THE THEME OF
OLD AGE

by

FRED PRATT GREEN

To the Staff
Residents and Friends
of
Cromwell House

Hope Publishing Company
CAROL STREAM, IL 60188

Stainer & Bell
LONDON

All royalties from sales of this book are donated to
The Methodist Homes for the Aged.

© 1991 Fred Pratt Green
First published in 1991 by
Hope Publishing Company, Carol Stream, Illinois 60188,USA
and
Stainer & Bell Limited, PO Box 110, 23 Gruneisen Road, London N3 1DZ, England

Previous publications by the same author:
This Unlikely Earth (out of print)
The Skating Parson (out of print)
The Old Couple (Peterloo Poets)
The Hymns and Ballads of Fred Pratt Green (Stainer & Bell/Hope)
Later Hymns and Ballads of Fred Pratt Green (Stainer & Bell/Hope)

British Library Cataloguing in Publication Data:
Green, Fred Pratt, 1903 —
 The last lap.
 I. Title
 821.914

ISBN: 0 85249 807 1 (World excluding USA and Canada)
ISBN: 0-916642-44-5 (USA and Canada)

Library of Congress Catalog Card Number: 91-076017

Printed in Great Britain by Galliard (Printers) Ltd, Great Yarmouth, England

CONTENTS

FOREWORD

"I still like a poem to be about an experience worth sharing", said Fred Pratt Green in a radio interview. This poet-parson is best known in church circles for the hymns he began writing when he retired from a distinguished pastoral and preaching ministry which had included such diverse appointments as East London during the Second World War and the Dome Mission, Brighton, besides service as Chairman of the Yorkshire and Hull District of the Methodist Church. In the United States, the Hymnal of the United Methodist Church contains more of his texts than those of any other living author.

Long before he took up hymnwriting as a second career, Fred Pratt Green gained recognition among those who read contemporary poetry for his sensitive handling of subjects like disablement and old age. Here we find the honest doubt which is the other side of the coin of faith in his corpus of hymnody. Here the Western Highlands of Scotland and the coast of Cornwall are recreated for our delight. Here religion which hast lost its joy is challenged. In all this work, Pratt Green's perceptive eye and mind delight and trouble us, sometimes delighting and troubling at one and the same time.

Just as we thought his writing days were over, the Reverend Dr. and Mrs Fred Pratt Green moved into a residential home and the author's sensitive eye and ear quickly tuned in to a new local world, and this volume of verse was born. Here are the insights of life's last lap.

BERNARD BRALEY

East Finchley, London
May 1991

INTRODUCTION

When we had to move out of our own home and seek security in a Methodist Home for the Aged, I had already decided that my writing days were over. At eighty-seven, I knew that old age does nothing for inspiration. The later work of Wordsworth is an example to all ageing poets. Of course, I had forgotten that Thomas Hardy corrects that hasty judgement.

As soon as I had settled into this community of old people, with its deserved reputation for caring, with its variety of personalities, sharpened rather than blunted by old age, with its pathos, its courage, its eccentricities, its incitement to gossip, its quiet fun and moments of hilarity, I began to feel that urge to write which I thought I had lost for ever.

So I began to write about the things that happen in our House, about what it means to live in this sort of community, sometimes to do more than report, to think of the deeper implications. Thus *A Sequence of Verse on a Theme of Old Age* took shape. I became very conscious of the need to be discreet, to avoid hurting feelings, and yet at the same time the need to be frank and honest. I hope I have succeeded. Where necessary, I have sought the goodwill of those most intimately concerned. I enjoyed writing these verses. I would like them to be enjoyed, even when one touches on what I have called 'the indignities of old age'.

I have called this a sequence of verse not of poetry, because I have in mind people who find poetry difficult and verse possible. I won't try to defend the distinction! Most pieces are written in the free style which is fashionable nowadays, but so like prose that many fail to see the difference. Fair enough! Read these pieces — some of which are in metre and rhyme — as naturally as you would read prose, but with a willingness to sense the rhythm, or varying rhythms, of the verse.

As for the title, *The Last Lap*, what I have in mind is not a competitive race but rather the finishing of a marathon, when winning doesn't matter but getting there does. Perhaps only the very elderly, and those under sentence of death earlier in life, can fully appreciate the significance of the Last Lap.

It should also be understood that *The Last Lap* does not imply finality. We Christians believe that the end we call death becomes a new beginning. We trust we shall find ourselves, refreshed and renewed and wiser, and entering upon a new First Lap, the nature of which is a mystery beyond our probing.

Finally, many thanks to those who, mostly without knowing it, helped me with these verses, especially to all at that Residential Home here called Oliver House.

FRED PRATT GREEN

Norwich
January 1991

The Last Lap

We were a long time making up our minds;
we must do so, we said, before winter.
Winters came and went. Nothing untoward
happened, so we were glad we had stayed,
enjoying another spring, another summer.

Old people, say the experts, should be cared for
by their neighbours, with the support of home-helps
and meals-on-wheels. Our neighbours are kind,
willing to put washers on taps, climb ladders,
but they, too, are no longer young. In the end

it was the garden made up our minds for us.
We had Andrew to cut the grass efficiently
for eight-pounds; but the annuals went unplanted,
the japonica unpruned; weeds defeated us.
To look out of the windows was to feel guilty.

Far-away relations sympathised; neighbours
were shocked, as if we had failed to trust them;
and Social Security (the resort of failures
and wasters?) answered some of our questions.
This is our Last Lap, I said, not too upset.

That you were upset did not surprise me,
for women strike deeper roots than men.
So we discussed, argued, almost quarrelled,
until, at last, my love, you conceded
that now our chief need is for security.

And security means living in community,
for us, certainly, a Home for the Aged;
and, after hestitation, the Home nearest
to us. Call it, for our present purpose,
not trying to disguise it, Oliver House.

Selling Up and Clearing The House

The decision once taken, selling up,
and clearing the house, hit us hard.
Retirement had been a change of trains,
a junction; this was a final journey
to a terminus, to a different life-style,
in two rooms, only eleven feet square.

Believing one way to fight depression
is to work, I set about the disposal
of books, then of unwanted possessions:
neglected silver, more than we expected;
forgotten treasure in unlikely places,
bric-a-brac, pretty but superfluous.

Before a next step could be taken,
the rooms had to be measured exactly,
spaces assessed, a bed here, a desk
either here or there, chairs a problem:
the guiding principle — less not more;
sentiment making choices difficult.

The process of selling-up, complicated
by the need to realise one's assets,
took time. A hundred partings left us
wounded, exhausted, but determined
to press on, until the end was reached.
We watched removal vans come and go.

Clearing the house of all that remained,
hardly worth an auctioneer's breath,
was like having a local anaesthetic.
Aware of finality, the tired mind
suspended its activities, still trusting,
with Mother Julian, all would be well.

4

First Impressions

A five-day, free visit
is a clever strategem
to see if they take to us,
and we take to them.

It is not our first visit
to Oliver House, but today
we see it in a new light,
think of it in a new way.

The site was large enough
for a two-storey spread,
thus sparing us the sensation
of being shut-in till dead.

Without wasting their money
on architectural frills
the planners gave us a Home
that admirably fulfils

its purpose. The entrance
is spacious and welcoming,
though visitors are warned,
politely, to ring the bell.

Essentials are to hand:
the office, visitors' loos:
and an In-and-Out board,
more neglected than in use.

On the right is the lounge,
and a room for prayer
and music; sensibly
the best piano is there.

Kitchen and dining-room
are first floor, to keep odours
from Reception, with a lift
for the disabled and infirm.

Each resident has a room,
small, cosy, with space to spare
for everything necessary
for our safety and welfare;

and if, after due warning,
we choke it with furniture,
and a clutter of memorabilia,
it's our own fault, to be sure.

Are first impressions best?
This place has the 'feel' of home,
that unspoken assurance
we would be made welcome.

6

Living in Community

One glorious week in the hot summer
Of Nineteen-Ninety, we began to live
in community. Having spent five days
in the House, to see if we liked it,
we were not strangers. This being Norfolk,
a region not famous for its hospitality,
our welcome was sincere but tentative.

Flowers from friends overflowed our rooms;
familiar objects, in their new setting,
look surprisingly at home. Both of us
felt reassured, but you, my dear, thought
that the outlook from your window,
of a flowerless bank and a wooden fence,
is unsightly. I have a glimpse of roses.

Living in community, we are warned,
can be damaging. A gain in security
must mean loss of freedom. Segregated
with the old, the disabled, the senile,
newcomers, though in reasonable health,
age quickly and lose interest in life.
We got the message. Now we take the risk.

There are thirty-five of us in residence;
not all of them are strangers to us. Soon,
we shall know them all, at close quarters:
their characters, infirmities, misfortunes;
likewise, under their critical scrutiny,
we ourselves will be known. But first,
we must survive a two-month trial.

On Trial

Being on trial is nothing new.
What trials, what examinations,
how many a vital interview,
we passed before we met at last;
and has not marriage been a test?
We also cry: 'Look! we have come through!'

Now, in old age, another test!
'A two-month trial period
is in everybody's interest . . .'
And if the answer were to be NO,
would we have to pack and go
back to a bare, abandoned nest?

A pure formality? Not so;
it puts us on our best behaviour,
makes us, I think, a little slow
to criticise, to form conclusions,
discourages the absurd illusions
people have of us before they know.

Rules and Regulations

Whether we like it or not, Oliver House
is an Institution as well as our Home:
and the disease most common to Institutions
is hardening of the arteries — I mean
over-regulation.
Take that hotel in Oban,
where the Proprietress made us welcome
by growling that as she and her husband
were cordon bleu, she had to insist
on our being prompt for meals. Day and night
we were threatened by Does and Donts!

It is not like that at Oliver House;
quite the opposite. The only Rules
that greeted us — behind the loo door —
were headed FIRE! Apart from meal times,
we only knew what instinct told us,
which wasn't much. So we had to ask:
what do we do when we want a bath?
or need a hair-cut? or chiropody?
The facilities for washing our smalls
are impressive, but what about sheets?
Is there a curfew? (Rumour has it
that residents at one Home are confined
to their rooms from 9 p.m. till breakfast!)
'Are we free to go out? to come in latish?'
'You ring the bell or ask for a key.'
We wondered about the religious aspect:
'No one is pressurised into praying.'

Our relaxed attitude is wonderful!
It turns an Institution into Home:
but one can see it is open to abuse.

The Ghost House

Remember it: but do not go back
to the house you have loved and left.
Ours, alas, has become a ghost house,
untenanted, unsold, neglected,
the garden we toiled in, kept trim,
in four months a wilderness,
no annuals planted, nothing pruned.

House martins were always welcome,
their nests in the deep eaves protected
against their miraculous return,
their excreta willingly expunged
like sins forgiven. Now nobody
forgives them, wiping the slate clean,
awaiting, with regret, their departure.

Our erstwhile neighbours are critical,
asking questions we cannot answer.
We hint at problems, express the hope
that everything will soon be put right;
perhaps when house-prices rise again,
and mortgages fall, the right persons
will inhabit the house we called home.

POSTSCRIPT

They say the house is sold. This is good news!
There are milk bottles on the doorstep.

Next-of-Kin

You can't imagine the trouble we're in,
having no accessible next-of-kin.

My wife, being an only child, is short
on relatives, and none of the right sort.

My nephew George, who's in Canada, can't
aid a relative so very distant;

as for my niece Marjorie, she's no nearer
at Polruan on the Cornish Riviera;

nor could I expect my nephew Victor
in London or Ireland, to be benefactor;

which is why I am asking my friend Ron,
who lives a mile away, to be the one

to act as next-of-kin, if the need
should arise. What need? and that indeed

is a question too awful to contemplate!
Only a fool, or a north country mate,

would accept such responsibility.
If this or that should happen, would he

be able to cope? We have the assurance
it has never happened, not even once!

My Cell

(with apologies to Robert Herrick)

Lord, Thou has given me a cell
wherein to dwell:
Thus sang a brother poet-cleric,
Robert Herrick,
in thankfulness to God for all
the blessings small,
and not so small, he fondly names,
from loaves to lambs.
His cell's a house *'whose humble roof*
is weatherproof;'
though mine's a cell eleven feet square,
there's room to spare
for loo and wardrobe, easy bed
well-blanketed,
three chairs, a footstool I shall keep
for daytime sleep,
a cabinet of steel to store
my hymns galore,
three pictures, all original,
to grace a wall,
a desk, with books of larger size
to make me wise,
gadgets to keep myself entire
should there be fire,
a table placed to get the light
both day and night,
a view not likely to distract
me from my act,
but colourful enough to please
myself at ease,
and all these things and more beside,
as Herrick cried:
'That I should render for my part
a thankful heart.'

Privacy

On a wall within reach
of anyone lying in bed
is a mysterious object
with four press-buttons.

One button is marked CALL,
a second is marked CANCEL,
a third says VOLUME,
The fourth says PRIVACY.

I expect if I press CALL
help will speedily arrive;
and if I change my mind
I must press CANCEL.

How by pressing a button
I get PRIVACY, no one
has been able to explain:
it's out of date, they say.

PRIVACY in a community
is a contradiction in terms;
or is it, I ask myself,
what we cannot do without?

It was then that I realised
how respectful we all are
of each other's privacy.
Our room is our refuge.

Against what? Against
too great a familiarity,
against having to conform
to the community norm.

Jobs and Chores

I have been given, by consent, a Job.
The distinction between Jobs and Chores
in my dictionary, is quite clear:
a Chore is menial; a Job, though humble,
has a status, a professional air.

Our Chore is the clearing of tables
after breakfast and tea on Tuesdays,
Thursdays and Saturdays. How a few
contrive to evade Chores is a lesson
in the art of looking the other way.

My Job is to collect the 'paper money'
on Saturdays after prayers. I sit,
like Matthew at the seat of custom,
in an attitude of confidentiality
(why are other people's jobs so funny?).

Actually, I am good at figures and
can add up without a calculator,
which nowadays even bank managers
find troublesome. It's being proffered
a ten-pound note for a single copy

of The People's Friend tests my nerve.
What intrigues me is who takes what.
I note with satisfaction that no one
is attracted to the Gutter Press:
we must be more cultured than I thought!

Hair Cut

Not to be excited would be inhuman!
In an improvised unisex salon
at the end of an ordinary corridor
I have my hair cut by a young woman.
There, seated on an ordinary chair,
I had to face an extraordinary sight:
two ladies, motionless as statues,
with horrid helmets on their heads.

Being used to a barber's mild routine
of comb and scissors working as a team,
painlessly taming my unruly hair,
followed by an aromatic spray,
I was shocked to have my locks seized
in fistfuls and dangerously scissored
by this Red Indian of a young woman
determined to go home with my scalp!

Perhaps, I pondered, a new life-style
calls for a new hair-style. Perhaps
it is not too late to explore a self
one could have been if life had taken
a different course. For my retirement
I bought pastels and studied Degas;
before I could enjoy fulfilment
or be disillusioned, the door closed.

The Other Side of the Fence (1)

What separates youth from age, for me,
is a rose-bed, a path, a strip of stones,
a bank of heather, and a wooden fence.

Sitting in my chair, pretending to read,
I can hear laughter and shouts,
mingled with soft thuds; youthful
heads move along the fence — and vanish.

A lad on the other side of the fence
is staring at me, but I cannot see
his expression, only half his face.

Does he know that we who live here,
on the other side of the fence,
are old people who end their lives here?
Perhaps he feels, in an immature way

old age concern? Moved by compassion
for him, for his endangered generation,
for its idealisms, its addictions,

I would have waved to him, hoping
to narrow the gap between us,
to share his world —   but he has vanished.
A school bell has ended our encounter.

The Other Side of The Fence (2)

We were rather slow at discovering
what remarkable things happen
on the other side of the fence;

perhaps not until the afternoon
we were told it was the Queen Mum
flying close in a red helicopter.

Then, one night, a yellow helicopter
(I may have got the colours confused)
flew by, lit up like a liner at sea.

In fact, the noise of helicopters
became so familiar an occurrence
we ceased to look up into the sky.

Would you believe it, but it makes sense,
there's a helicopter-pad
on the other side of our fence!

But why in the grounds of a school?
Because it's the best open space
close to the City Centre and the Hospital.

Here it comes! We watch it descend
this time, noisier than ever,
for what purpose? what emergency?

Has there been another accident
on a North Sea rig? Or is it a case
only our hospital can treat?

These questions trouble us a little
as the helicopter drops out of sight.
We shall never know which guess was right.

On Not Feeding The Gulls

The house-martins have all gone,
but the gulls are back from the sea;
an exchange is no robbery.

Hunting their food on the wing,
the martins make no demands,
except to nest in the eaves.

But the gulls are back from the sea,
shamelessly begging for food,
their spotters on roof and aerial.

Throw them a fistful of bread:
before you can dodge indoors
they'll be on the lawn — and away!

A friend of mine used to say:
'Their proper place is the sea;
let them beg there, if they must!'

The gulls are back from the sea;
alas, I've nothing to give them,
not even the stalest crust.

A Walk in the Paradise Garden

Perhaps not paradise exactly;
but in this urban survival
of Edwardian domesticity
our garden is a private place
for exercise, reverie, peace.

As I sit at my window, writing,
old ladies pass by, some pushed
in wheel-chairs by caring staff,
some with frames, or without aid:
not knowing me well enough to wave.

So, following their good example.
and taking my stick, I too walk
in our paradise garden, noting
that the tree mallow is untidy,
its luxuriant flowering over.

Everywhere there are signs
of the harm done by the drought.
Suddenly, walking on the burnt grass,
I stumble. Heads are turned;
there would be help if I needed it.

With these feet, I tell myself,
I used to climb Helvellyn
by Striding Edge, afraid
of the double precipice, daring
myself to conquer timidity.

Tired, I am glad of the shade
of the tallest pine in Norfolk;
scattered about, in shadow
and sunshine, other residents
are nodding off, peacefully.

Someone is broadcasting Mozart;
ideally it should be Delius
on this day of oppressive heat,
or Debussy's dreamy evocation
of how a faun spent an afternoon.

Garden Party

How English a Garden Party is!
Alas, after a hot, dry summer
our lawns are a pitiable sight;
even the croquet hoops wilt.

Is this why our garden party
lacks liveliness? why side-shows
do badly, and people drift away?
Cakes and woolly toys do best.

The Friends of the House mingle
with us. Their care for us
is constant and practical;
they run our well-stocked shop.

Garden parties tend to be demure.
There should be morris-dancing;
we have eurythmics instead.
What a pity it is so hot!

Excitement at last! Children,
with their lively young mums,
burst upon us. Of course,
this is what has been missing!

Our greatest lack here, I think,
is children under our feet,
getting into mischief, unaware
that old people are getting older.

Rainbow

It was while we were at breakfast,
one day in October,
someone noticed it:
a rainbow of astonishing beauty
spanning our rain-washed city.
Some craned their necks to see it,
several, talking of rainbows,
went to the windows,
while others, lacking interest,
went on eating their breakfast.
And I remembered a night
on a cruise to the Canaries,
when the captain himself
called us on deck
to see a rarity, a moonbow.
What we saw was a silver arc
on the distant horizon,
so mysterious, so beautiful,
none of us said anything at all.

Caring

Caring is a word I am weary of,
a word as slick and abused as love:

caring is awareness of a genuine need,
caring is knowing when not to heed;

caring is firmness without being cross,
caring is sharing another's loss;

caring is support for the lame and blind,
caring is patience with a failing mind;

caring is calmness in a time of stress,
is keeping cool when clearing up a mess;

caring is unshocked by guilt or shame,
caring is loving by another name;

caring is not a one-sided virtue,
caring is trust when the carers hurt you.

Without caring, worlds fall apart,
and chaos reigns, as at the start.

The Indignities of Old Age

A Resident speaks

How shall I describe it?
The body no longer knows
how to behave itself;
it functions irresponsibly,
it acts out of character.
Others have to take charge.

Of those who take charge
all are kind; one or two
are more clumsily kind
than others, handling us
as if we were sacks of coal.
It used to irritate me;
now I can joke about it.

Often, looking at the youngest,
the one who is a Trainee,
I wonder if at seventeen
I would have been willing
to commit myself to sharing
the indignities of old age.

God answers Job

When old age robs us of our dignity,
when under stress of age affections fray,
when wrinkled features threaten to betray
a self less kind, or dread disease sets free
an alien, uncontrolled identity:
I will not look! I turn my face away!
I hate the God, to whom I have to pray,
for doing things like this to you and me.

'Hold on!' cries God, who has another Job
upon his hands: 'How can you hope to probe
the mysteries of my unique creation?
This is the final test, the last temptation,
to lose your grip on My integrity.'
I yield! His word is good enough for me.

Medications

In this matter of medication
we are a privileged people,
who no longer must walk
to a mile-away clinic
for our Navidrex-K.

Here every affliction
to which old age is prone
(except that of ageing),
has its pill or potion
guaranteed not to kill.

Do you need Bisacodyl,
or even Digoxin?
You'll not get it ad lib:
your tablets are fated to be
recorded and dated.

So it's rather perplexing,
as we get up from breakfast,
if, shaken by dismay
you say: 'Have I taken
my Navidrex-K?'

Fire!

Our fire alarm is deafening;
it has to be to waken the deaf,
to penetrate the remotest room.

Everyone is falling out of bed,
dragging on a warm garment,
erupting into the corridor.

Already the safety doors
dividing the corridors
have sealed us off.

Someone has forgotten dentures,
someone has forgotten slippers,
someone has forgotten a handbag
(you don't need a handbag, dear).

Are the windows all shut?
Is anyone still in bed?
Can anyone smell smoke?

Sorry! it's gone off in error!
They ought to have an all-clear
(too much like the war, dear).

It's two o'clock in the morning:
if only the tea-trolley
would trundle into sight!

Good night, ladies,
good-night,
good-night, Mr. T. S. Eliot.

Night-Watch

Shortly after midnight,
and shortly after four:
a slowly opened door,
a narrow strip of light.

It's the night staff making sure
he's all right in Number Ten:

is he doubled up with pain?
has he fallen out of bed?
is he prematurely dead?

If I'm awake, I say:
don't worry, I'm O.K.

Oh, angels of the night,
it strikes me that I might
be doubled up in pain,
or have fallen out of bed,
or be prematurely dead.

Tonight I had to say:
God bless you! I'm O.K.

Nocturne

Coming home (it is home now)
at the late hour of eleven,
to a locked door and a house
in almost total darkness,
it seemed to me, for a moment,
to be a ship riding at anchor
in a land-locked harbour,
the captain, mate and crew,
except for the night-watch,
fast asleep in their bunks.
Having a key in my pocket,
I unlocked the door, entered,
and recorded myself as IN.
From somewhere in the semi-darkness
the night-watch appeared,
to check up on me. A ship,
I thought, riding at anchor,
all of us asleep in our bunks...
Suddenly, a call for help
rang out urgently. With a smile
the night-watch hurried off to meet
the night's first emergency.

Infra~Structure

The personnel of Oliver House
may be said to comprise
    Senior Staff
    Caring Staff
    Night Staff
    Cleaning Staff
    Kitchen Staff

Our Cook does wonders every day
except the day we have fish
(she is allergic to the smell)
when the Assistant Cook takes over.
And in this female world, a Handyman:
how many things we cannot do, he can!

The personnel of Oliver House
may also be said to comprise
    Relief Staff
    Trainees

This division of the Infra-Structure
collapses intentionally when
there's a shortage of staff
    or an emergency
    when almost everyone
is expected to do everyone else's job
    thus the Cleaner becomes a Carer
    and a Carer becomes Senior Staff.

The total effect, surprisingly,
is of order not chaos. Surely
such a happy and efficient staff
must themselves be a happy family.
    Only they know!

Matron

The word still casts its spell
of starched authority
on relics of a by-gone age
like me:
of Roman matriarchs,
so virtuous and bold
the greatest Caesars had to do
as they were told:
of Matrons I have met,
when visiting the wards,
with whom, alas, I did not dare
to bandy words;
and, frightful memory!
that Matron of my school
we could not fool,
who dosed us with cod-liver oil.
How strange, so late in life,
to have to face once more
a Matron, but with wider powers
than those of yore;
and find beneath authority
what every Matron ought to be:
friendly, cheerful, efficient, knowing
what to do and when
for intransigent old men,
and helpless old women.

Tea-Trolley

We hear it first in the distance,
　　the music a trolley makes
as it shudders and shakes,
　　reviving the joys of existence.

It's the Matron! she's on her way
　　with a cheery 'good morning!' and pills
to cure all our ills
　　and the very first cup of the day.

In mid-morning, a Junior Staff
　　will be teaching a younger Trainee
the dispensing of tea,
　　with a mixture of laughter and chaff.

A Deputy-Matron, no less,
　　wakes the somnolent afternoon
with tinkle of spoon,
　　and cups handed out with finesse.

At eight in the evening, a cuppa,
　　with biscuits, is served in the lounge,
unless you can scrounge
　　something more for a secretive supper.

When my life seems at last to be ending,
　　one sound will be heaven to me:
a trolley with tea;
　　and I'll cry: 'I'm not dying, I'm mending!'

The Importance of Meals

'The time to see them best is when they feed
the animals' is very true indeed
of us! but not at breakfast when we eat,
in semi-consciousness, our prunes or wheat-
abix, and only come alive when made
to pile the plates or pass the marmalade.

At lunch, which we call dinner, we feel free
to air our views and gossip cheerfully
before the Grace, and after, as we wait
to see what Providence has put upon our plate
(the food is better than at most hotels).
Between the courses, too, are intervals
for talk, as tables, checking irritation,
wait to be served, in very strict rotation.

Tea is a simpler meal, with ample time
for talk of relatives, or church, or crime;
and drink and biscuits in the lounge at eight
prove few are anxious to associate
when a soap-opera is on the air —
disrupt our darling pastime, if you dare!

One thing is most important: who sits where;
deciding this is Matron's constant care.
To sit with friends at breakfast, dinner, tea,
may seem desirable to you and me,
but not to Matron, who must try to fix
the seating so we get a social mix,
and yet contrive to find a place for those
who must be helped, and even juxtapose,
either by accident, or just for fun,
persons suspected of not getting on.
Dear Matron, if we ask why So-and-So
is where she is, you tactfully reply:
'In six weeks time I'll have another try.'

Green-Side-Up

Our place-mats are a credit to the House,
depicting Pheasant, Ptarmigan and Grouse,
and have a most imaginative use:

if anyone is eating out,
They turn the place-mat green-side up,
and no one is in any doubt.

They've turned the place-mat green-side up,
and everyone knows why:
she's gone to Oberammergau
to see the Passion Play.
They've turned the place-mat green-side-up
and everyone knows why:
he's gone to see his relatives
in Hereford and Hay.

O we know we mustn't worry,
and we really do try:
but they've turned the place-mat green-side-up
and nobody knows why:
and the secret thought is troubling me:
do they turn the place-mat green-side-up
the day we die?

Jam-Butties

At tea-time, as if it were a ritual,
bread-butter-jam is on the menu,
though, in fact, few of us eat it.

I am reminded of the jam-butties
of working-class Lancashire:
the bread in hunks, with marge scrape,
if you were lucky; the plum jam
home-made, with a ritual seed-cake
on Sundays, when between school and chapel
we feasted, the big kettle singing
on the hob, welcoming visitors.

I remember, too, the Edwardian teas
of my childhood: the dainty sandwiches
of egg-and-cress or of cucumber;
and the thinnest of bread-and-butter,
to be eaten, oh not, my dear, with jam
but home-made *preserve*, cherry
perhaps; and on a three-tier stand
buttered scones, plain and fancy cakes,
and, as a centre-piece, a fruit-cake,
partly cut; the tea-service silver,
the china Crown Derby, on Sundays.

Tomorrow, perhaps, I will decline ham,
and be content with bread, butter and jam.

Admonitions

Is everything sweetness and light
    in this wonderful Home of ours?
To expect it would be to forget
    not everyone says it with flowers.

So if Matron's forgotten your pills,
    and the carers don't care if you're dead,
don't count the few times you've been missed,
    count your blessings instead.

If your portion of pie is too small,
    and the honey's a brand you don't like,
ask yourself why on earth our providers
    haven't all gone on strike.

If Beethoven's Ninth's just a noise
    that prevents you from going to sleep,
why not thank the Creator for music
    as you count every sheep?

If you find yourself neighbour at meals
    to the person you cannot abide,
what a chance as you pass the pepper
    to find that appearances lied.

If the talk is ten minutes too long,
    and you wish you were back in bed,
God is preaching — his text is patience —
    as saintly George Herbert said.

Television

In the beginning, twenty years ago,
this was the Television Room.
At the popular hours of broadcasting
residents crowded into it,
anxious to view favourite programmes,
learning the chief lesson of community.

Now our impressive television set
is antiquated and unused,
a useful surface for surplus ornaments,
in what is now the Prayer Room.
Knowledgeable people view it critically:
it may soon be a valuable asset.

Today we have television in our rooms;
in the age of the video,
how could it be otherwise? The price paid
is a change in social behaviour:
though we now spend most of our time apart,
what can we do to preserve our privacy?

Stand tonight in one of our long corridors
and listen! How many programmes
are fused into that confusing of sound?
One by one they are silenced.
A last viewer sleeps in front of the box
to the strains of Rock, until someone knocks.

Visitors

Relatively speaking, few of us
are alone in the world:
others have friends and relatives
who can't leave us alone;
but others have visitors who know
what needs to be done.

Imagine the daughter from London
who, at dinner-time,
descends on the House with complaints
her mother's neglected,
that nothing's been done for her asthma,
well, nothing expected.

Imagine the grandson from Wales
who goes out of his way,
when surfing at Southend-on-Sea,
to look up the old dear,
and takes her to lunch, in his banger,
and drives with due care.

Imagine the friend from the past
who, instead of flowers,
brings her the bed-socks she's knitted,
and photos she meant to destroy,
and a packet of somebody's shortbread
they used to enjoy.

Going To Church in a Mini-Bus

Going to church in our useful mini-bus
is a strange experience for some of us,
as if it were insufficiently pious.

We might be off to Yarmouth or Cromer
for a day's excursion in high summer,
armed with sandwiches and in good humour.

There's the same unease: is everyone here?
the disposition to greet with a cheer
late-comers when they deign to appear;

the same fuss about who shall sit where,
the grumbles and pleasantries, and an air
of being stranded neither here nor there.

Of course, we are all suitably attired,
all striving to feel suitably inspired,
not all adjusted to the mood required.

Perhaps they were this in Chaucer's time,
on pilgrimage to some exotic shrine,
mixing the incongruous with the sublime.

A Storm in a Tea-Cup

With a new crisis threatening
war somewhere in the world,
only faint echoes of which reach
these distant and misty shores,
we have our own sharp dispute.

The row is about our lounge chairs.
We like them arranged in circles
(to be more correct: elliptically)
thus encouraging conversation
and an air of informality.

However, in the hours of darkness,
someone shifts them into rows
facing each other. The effect
is suggestive of railway carriages
of quite intimidating rigidity.

This, they say, is how it used to be,
though now it seems undesirable:
why should sitting in our lounge
become a journey on British Rail
to nowhere in particular?

The mystery is: who is it shifts
these easy but cumbersome chairs
while we sleep? Not the staff,
we are assured. Perhaps a past
resident with poltergeistic powers?

By keeping a strict surveillance
of the lounge at likely times
we have caught her red-handed:
a highly regarded, deaf old lady
with a strong sense of what is right.

Doing Nothing

Today, I want to do nothing:
doing nothing
is very easy in this place.

That is why those who care for us
like to arrange
activities of all kinds:
    entertainments musical
    and otherwise;
    craft and keep-fit classes;

    coffee mornings for charity,
    Bible classes,
    carpet-bowls and croquet;

    outings to Cromer and Yarmouth,
    to nature reserves,
    zoos and Sandringham.

Television is a good way
of doing nothing
when everything else fails.

Doing nothing, I observe,
is only boring
when there is nothing to do.

Today, I want to do nothing
because of things
I am supposed to want to do.

Cromwell

Let me introduce you to Cromwell,
not that he appreciates attention,
except from a few privileged persons.

Cromwell is a black cat, and beautiful,
black-hearted, aloof, and disdainful
of humans who, in need of affection,

try to possess him. A sudden scratch
settles that! Even genuine cat lovers
give up, concealing their hurt feelings.

Worse is to come! It must be confessed
that Cromwell is a dedicated hunter,
not of mice, which would be praiseworthy,

but of birds — not starlings, comedians
of the garden, too clever to be caught —
but of fledging sparrows and thrushes;

even blackbirds, perpetually in panic,
do not escape Cromwell's wicked claws,
No wonder we support the R. S. P. B.

Why is he called Cromwell? That's easy!
Look at him now, stalking through the lounge,
his tail in the air, ignoring us all,

the very image of Independency!

Budgerigars

How beautiful they are, one green, one blue!
Birds in cages, doesn't it trouble you?
Doesn't it set 'all heaven in a rage',
to see two budgies in a cage?
And is it psychologically fair
to cage two males, as though they are a pair?

How beautiful they are, one blue, one green!
How charmingly they bob about, and preen,
and peck each other, in assault or play,
nudge the bright bell or make the bauble sway!
They must be pleased with their captivity:
Cromwell would catch them if we set them free.

We love to hear their chatter — most of us;
but some complain the noise is hideous,
worse than some human voices, 'you know whose!'
So covered up by yesterday's bad news,
they sulk in silence as we say our prayers;
or, do you think, they may be saying theirs?

Apology To The Very Deaf

It was obvious you were deaf.
Using the mask of cheerfulness,
smiling, making jokes, you hid
from us the unacceptable truth
that you had heard nothing!

Do you wonder we were vexed?
Even the simplest conversation
proved impossible; and when
we tried poking you with words
you got hold of the wrong end

of the stick. We try to fathom
why you are behaving like this.
It could be pride, a face-saving
exercise. No! it isn't that —
then what? We believe we know.

The truth is: you hate fuss,
you don't want to embarrass us;
the pretence is for our sakes.
We all love you for it. Tell us:
do we persevere? or give up?

A Little Lady

Here she comes, the little lady,
so very bent, so fragile,
so dependent on her stick,
so determined: a miracle!

They say her niece Angela
chooses her dresses. Cosy,
elegant and colourful,
they are always in fashion.

Her hair, too, is a miracle:
a soft grey, it frames a face
gentle, unravaged by age.
We know she is nearly blind.

After cutting up her food for her,
I am fascinated by the way
she handles a spoon, careful
not to offend good manners.

Here she comes, at ninety-four,
grasping her stick firmly,
but more agitated than usual
because she thinks she is late.

Standing behind her chair,
to settle her at the table,
I am prouder than a footman
at a Guildhall banquet.

A Surprising Story

Like a small bird with a bright plumage,
she's so distinctive you can't miss her;
and if, sitting next to her at dinner,
you show willingness to attend to her,
she may tell you her surprising story.

She lived as a child in St. Petersberg,
where her father, a British industrialist,
was sustaining the Russian war effort.
Suddenly the Bolsheviks seized power,
and the family were in extreme danger.

With civil war raging in the streets,
and a German army almost within sight,
they fled by the only route to freedom,
by train to Finland, taking with them
whatever valuables they were able to save.

On that frightening journey to safety
their train was attacked by Bolsheviks
or brigands, and the passengers stript
of everything except the clothes they wore.
Eventually they escaped to England.

What an experience for a child of eight!
Do you wonder she repeats her story?
And here she is, in her infirm old age
sustaining an elegance, an aloofness,
it would be insensitive to resent.

A Tall Lady

How straight she is, as if to shame
the frailty which must use a frame,
surviving all who lack the will
to weather every human ill;
and ready, if the time has come,
to move into a larger room.

Behind her, hollyhocks along a wall,
flowerless now, and eight feet tall,
await the gardener's tidying up,
in certain hope of next year's crop.

Progress Backwards

I cannot believe my eyes!
She emerged from her room
backwards. yes! backwards
in her versatile wheel-chair,
into the long corridor
I have nicknamed The Strand;
then, letting the door gently fall to
she turned the corner, backwards,
and skilfully using the handrails
propelled herself at high speed
to the obliging lift,
enjoying her athleticism.
'Madam,', I said. 'I arrest you
for breaking the speed-limit
in a built-up area, and
for driving a vehicle in reverse,
without a proper licence,
to the danger of the public!'
Of course, what I meant was:
'I award you a gold medal
for courage in overcoming disability,
for making progress backwards,
and for a special kind of humour.

When we were Young

When we were young, a boy became a Scout,
a girl a Guide, with badges to be won,
and Mafeking was still within a shout:
we had no doubt what life was all about.

When we were young, we counted every run,
and cheered whoever hit a mighty six;
we played our friendly cricket in the sun,
and never doubted sport was chiefly fun.

When we were young, and houses were to let,
and mortgages transactions of the rich,
when credit cards had not been thought of yet,
we had no doubt the enemy was debt.

When we were young, we had a steady thirst
for skills that were the gateways to success:
so for the best of us, as for the worst,
we never doubted basics must come first.

Now we are old, what troubles us the most
is that our standards have been overthrown:
forgive us if we feel a little lost,
and wonder if your world is worth the cost.

Bonnets and Perms

A woman in my grandmother's time
began, at sixty, to wear a bonnet;
and, because she wore it, she felt old,
as old as the Empire's widowed Queen.

What, I wonder, is today's symbol
of feminine old age? I glance discreetly
at our old ladies. How well they dress!
How beautifully permed their white hair!

It is almost as though having a perm
is a refusal to submit to old age,
despite the wheel-chair and the frame,
a shortness of breath and arthritis.

And why not? We wage eternal war
against Father Time. It's a losing battle,
but one, paradoxically, we must win;
not to believe this, is to be defeated.

Sex in Old Age

A banner headline
in the Better Press:
SEX IN OLD AGE:
I ignored the page.

Late in my eighties,
I have to confess
I am quite content,
all passion spent,

whatever is offered
of delight or stress,
to ignore the page:
SEX IN OLD AGE.

Then, impelled to savage
the Better Press
for soiling the morn
with soft porn,

I read the page,
but found nothing amiss
and much good sense
in SEX IN OLD AGE.

It's on the table
for anyone able,
today, to read it —
if they should need it!

Old Age ~ The Leveller

A prospective resident put the question:
'What is the proportion of men to women?'
I had to answer: 'Four men to thirty women.'
He received my admission in grim silence.

I felt I had to be strictly truthful:
'And of the four men, three are parsons.'
This did little to make him more cheerful.
'Old age,' I ventured, 'is a great leveller.'

So it is! Old men turn into old women.
What matters is not a matter of sex,
rather the fact you are going deaf and blind,
or need help in the middle of the night.

A parson here is a person who needs help.
My questioner nodded. 'As a bachelor,'
he complained, 'I am very vulnerable.'
To this, I felt, there was no polite answer.

The Paradox of Age

The average age here is eighty-seven;
I am in my eighty-eighth year.
The paradox of age fascinates me.
For the purpose of this discussion
we can be divided into three groups:
the Seventies, the Eighties, the Nineties.

the Seventies, relatively, are young;
they should be our eager activists;
the Eighties, mature and experienced,
the leaders of our community;
the Nineties, in feebleness extreme,
the chief objects of our compassion.

Of course, it is not like this at all!
The Nineties are quite resiliant;
our oldest inhabitant, at ninety-nine,
walks round the garden without a frame;
our best speech-maker is ninety-five.
Age, here, has little significance.

Mozart was a mature musician
at fifteen, or earlier. Hardy
write his best poetry in old age.
Today, remarkably, I feel younger
in some ways, than in adolescence.
Tomorrow, I may need a wheel-chair.

Time

Time here, for some of us,
is morning, noon, night.
What day of the week it is,
what month of the year it is,
what year, eludes us quite.

On the edge of Eternity
we have lost track of time.
Some are too deaf to hear,
in their cocoon of silence,
a clock's insistent chime.

Relieved of responsibility,
with no dead-line to beat,
it takes a clanging handbell,
and a thump on the door
to tell us it's time to eat.

Time has stolen the years
from us. Now, defying Time,
we are happy, recapturing
the long-ago, absent-
mindedness our only crime.

The Vital Question

However unlike we are
in sex, age, temperament,
there is something we all share;
we are travellers to Eternity,
    and nearly there.

Our journey has been different
in landscape and circumstance;
yet in the end we all went
to the self-same destination,
    the same event.

The event is this very day
in Norwich, our fine city,
where, for a short or longer stay,
we have all become actors
    in the same play

But does the Author leave us free,
within an open-ended plot,
to share his creativity?
If so, how little time is left
    to you and me.

Religion

That this is a religious House is true;
but not in the monastic sense. We own
allegiance to a Church that does not frown
on any enterprise that keeps in view
the love of Christ for all humanity.
Was not our founder, Wesley, catholic
in his contentious age, himself so quick
to see a need and find a remedy?

Religion here is neither hot nor cold,
which, despite Laodicea, I confess
suits my desire, in dotage, for toleration.
What is the use, I ask, of growing old
if we've not learned that truth is manifold,
and caring a chief part of our vocation?

A Death in the House

One day there will be a death in the House.
If this troubles us, it is only in secret:
why worry about dying. What is the use?

One day this year there will be a celebration,
God willing, when one of us is an hundred:
she will receive the Queen's congratulations.

It is surprising how the frailest survive,
so no one knows who will be next to go;
and there are those who do not wish to live.

Faith, or fortitude alone, sustains us
in these years of facing the inevitable,
some hoping for Heaven or for release.

'When there is a death in the House, how
will it affect us?' I got the answer:
'There will be silence rather than sorrow.'

A silence may say more than ritual words;
a sense of gratitude may transcend grief,
for in death, as in life, we are the Lord's.